Matisse:

Messages from a Soul

(September 2006–April 2008)

By Khittah A. Wolven (CWR, Ally Brody)

Cover Art by Gina Charles

©A.E. Brody 2011 to 2020

©Khittah A. Wolven 2020

© Cernu Wolf Raven 2014 to 2020

©Ally Brody 2012 to 2020

Table of Contents

4

5

Forgotten Names

Forgotten Feelings

Forgotten Knowledge

Forgotten Words

Forgotten Vision

Forgotten Changes

Forgotten Thoughts

Forgotten Paths

Forgotten Plea

Forgotten Poem

Forgotten Summons

Forgotten Decision

Forgotten Oath

Forgotten Looking

Forgotten Spell

Forgotten Keeping

Heart Messages

Swan

Opossum

Moose

Turtle

Coyote

Wolf

Snake

Eagle

Mountain Lion

Armadillo

Whale

Dolphin

Raccoon

Frog

Antelope

Lizard

9

Blue Heron

Spider

Grouse

Jaguar

Hawk

Fox

Horse

Owl

Weasel

Prairie Dog

Bat

Mouse

Ant

Crow

Deer

Giraffe

Kangaroo

Koala

Lion

Lynx

Porcupine

Otter

Rabbit

Seal

Butterfly

Cougar

Raven

I am

Protection Messages – Three Times– July 2007

Dream Messages Series

Nightmare

General Messages

Sides

Red eyes, Black eyes, Blue eyes watching, Knowing, Not knowing. Angelic, Demonic, Vampiric eyes Waiting, Not waiting. Fighting In the shadows, In the light.

Raven and Ram As animal spirits. The Raven as the dominant one Of the heart. One for mystery, Raven. One for sacrifice, Ram.

All watching and waiting to see Which way fate falls Either in Darkness or in Light But only victory for one side.

By Ally Brody (KAW)

Passover

Busy bustling around the kitchen For one of the fourth busiest Holidays in the year. Its a little rest here and a lot of work there.

Making matzah ball soup the way Mom-Mom makes it. But for a family tradition, Everyone needs to help now and then.

For the night will come upon us fast, And the celebration of The fleeing of Egypt will begin.

By Ally Brody (KAW)

Dreams

Tarot and Gypsy Cards tell me that;

I fell in love long ago. I must act to find him. I will meet him in the rain. His appearance is dark and romantic looking.

I shall marry eventually But it will be someone I have not yet met Under snowy hills. My days shall end in a Utopian community. I was in danger Physically and emotionally, or spiritually but it is over now.

And with any profession I follow, I will always be an amateur.

So, here waiting And here staying Until I can go and look For him that is my mate And dream dreams Those only dreamers can About who he is, What he looks like, And what he does.

All the while, Real life is saying Stop dreaming of what could be. While I am waiting to be free To look and take action To find the one meant for me.

By Ally Brody (KAW)

Wind Call

The wind calls As it blows through The leaves in the trees The wind calls As it ripples through

Fields To his sister:

Come, Come, Time is nigh.

I call as I walk, I call as I run, Back to him:

Soon Soon I know, but I will come soon.

As I always say.

By Ally Brody

Wind Calls by Allison E. Brody aka AEB

Soul Wanderer

Soul Wanderer, you go wandering everywhere Going place to place but always Returning To the place of Origin. What do you seek?

I seek the place where he is.

What are you running from?

What am I running from?

Where are you running to?

I run to where my heart leads me. I run to an unknown place.

What are you protecting?

I protect all of those I call pack. I protect everyone who cares for me. I protect everyone who I care for. Wandering everywhere.

By Ally Brody (KAW)

Darkness

Stalking far away, Silently watching. Like a predator with its prey, Consuming everything in its path. Till it comes to the barrier of light Surrounding the prey.

Now it's waiting Watching For the day When the protection is gone.

By Ally Brody

Summer Day

Sun as bright and warm as it can be. Forest as cool as a summer's breeze. Wine as ripe as different berries. Wine as tart as raspberries. Wine as sweet as strawberries. Night as warm as a thunderstorm.

By Ally Brody (KAW)

Rain

It washes away Pain, sorrow, hurt, and betrayal.

It brings Renewal, new life, hope And Brings sorrowful memories. Tears come and Raindrops are Icy tears that are never shed.

By Ally Brody

Grampy I

It rained the day he died. It rained on the day of his funeral. In peace he died. At peace he is. Welcomed into the light With the open arms of the Lord.

His animal spirit is a frog. Frog symbolizes New life, Rebirth, Feminine energy, Fecundity, And creation.

Grandfather, Father, Husband, Democratic Mayor, Director
of Public Office, Army Man.

By Ally Brody

Elements of Nature

Wood to Earth, Earth to Fire, Fire to Air, Air to Water,

Water to Wood, Wood to Spirit, Earth to Spirit, Fire to Spirit,
Air to Spirit, Water to Spirit, Spirit to Metal.

Metal to Iron, Iron to Steel Steel to Copper, Copper to
Bronze, Bronze to Silver, Silver to Gold, Gold to Metal,

Metal to Fire, Fire to Earth.

By Ally Brody

Unknown I

Crying, Cleansing, Drowning, Raining down. Remembering
the past, Knowing the future, Changing the present, Trying

to change the future While trying to show The truth in small ways. Falling To keep others up. Numbing, Feeling, Rain.

By Ally Brody

Unknown II

Drowning, Falling Down. Swimming. Flying, Soaring High. Light to find, Dark for comfort.

By Ally Brody

My Heart's Language

Nayea, No tisa Ca Mi sonya. Miyata Niheya Coneya.

Translation:

Shadows, do not take of my soul. Light and Darkness Combined.

By Ally Brody

Unknown III

Protecting, Guiding, Teaching, Guarding. Two I'm doing, Two I'm trying to do But always I have a Wolf-like Heart.

By Ally Brody

Kundalini

Snake Coiling, Awakening, Building, Energizing, Healing, Holy Fire

By Ally Brody

Fire Spirit

The Blessed, Holy, Heaven Fire is the Holy Spirit. The Damned, Demon, Hell Fire is a dark spirit unknown to us.

Once they were one and the same, Now they are split in two. But together they make up The Sacred Flame, Sacred Fire.

They are a part of each other. They are sister and brother. When you summon one, You summon the other.

Both of fire. Both are spirits. Both are fire spirits. Both are angels. Both are demons.

They are split between two masters. One master fights with the light. The other master fights with the darkness. While both masters can be of light or darkness.

One of the fire spirits is of life, The other one is of death. When one is of protection, The other is of harm. While one is of peace, The other is of chaos.

When the holy fire dies a final time, All Protection will cease. Then demon fire will reign, And the apocalypse will begin.

By Ally Brody

Red-eyed Snake

Oh, Golden one, With your ruby eyes! Oh, King of snakes, Protector and guardian of The source of spiritual life.

Could you open and speak for me, And tell what wisdom there is to tell? Oh, Friend! Will you share what upon the world there is to share? For nothing could acknowledge you.

If truth were but a single word, Could you share it with me, Someday?

By Ally Brody

Snake Painting By Allison E. Brody aka AEB

Mystery

To see the darkness All around, Creeping closer All the time. To feel darkness Consuming life. To know that It is coming for you, That the end will come When you die. But while Not seeing, feeling, or knowing All these things That are what the Spirits know But keep Hidden For us to find.

By Ally Brody

Secret

Flying so high, Falling so fast. And all the time Seeing and knowing What will be. With knowledge and Mystery, Sacrifice and strife In many ways All can be Hidden.

By Ally Brody

Faith and Mom

Damn me. Bless me. Love me. Hate me. I'm confused about your feelings For me Because of what your actions show.

You accept me Yet ignore my beliefs. You say that I'm a saint. Yet being biased to me by saying That I don't know what being Christian is. Saying that I don't sacrifice That I indulge.

But that's calling the kettle black When I sacrifice more of my soul Each day trying to keep loving When I barely get anything back.

By Ally Brody

Souls

Old and new, Ancient and young, Life and death Combined Within one. When the End of days come All is released, All is awakened.

By Ally Brody

Energy

Healing, Swirling, Tingling Warmth. Drained away Or full up Healing us Physically, Mentally, Emotionally And spiritually.

By Ally Brody

Forgotten Memories Series

Forgotten Prayer

I Pray to Jesus, my brother, That you will understand

And think about what I say And what I write. A telling of my love Though I have never seen him But in my dreams.

Tell me what you seek to hide In your memory and in your heart.

May my brother Watch over you And protect you from harm Always until you die. You felt something on the Night of a full moon. Focus on it, Feel it again. For it might tell you Something you might not believe.

By Ally Brody

Forgotten Knowing

I am getting shrouded In a mist of mystery. Mystery in the past. A connection to the present.

I'm hungry. I'm very hungry spiritually. I'm hungry physically. I'm thirsty. I'm very thirsty spiritually. I'm thirsty physically.

By Ally Brody

Forgotten Dreams

The castle with the vampire Who calls me Changeling.

Christ, Lord, Jesus, Brother Talking to a wolf about me.
Talking to a timber wolf about me In a forest. These
dreams, the things I dream about and others Seem so real
to me.

The castle on the hill. My prince, my vampire, lived there. I
must find the secret passage That leads to him.

By Ally Brody

Forgotten Calling

Come to me, Wind. Come to Changeling. Come to me.

Wolves call me In the wind saying

Come home to us, Changeling. Come home to us.

He calls to me In the wind saying

Come to me, Changeling. Come to me.

By Ally Brody

Forgotten Names

Water or rain of any form, Lauren. Wind of any form, Natasha. Fire, thunder, lightning, or electricity Of any form, Allison, Me.

By Ally Brody

Forgotten Feelings

It seems like I am having The life drained out of me.

I need to talk to someone I need someone to listen.

I need someone to understand. I need someone to help me.

I am loved. I know in my heart. But what am I loving? Is it something that is real or a dream? The emptiness is growing from not being loved.

Daydreams of my love, Dreams of my love. A connection between Him and me.

By Ally Brody

Forgotten Knowledge

A fire of hatred In the center and root Of her heart of fire of love. She should accept What she is in her heart.

I know that sister has a heart of fire of love. A fire of love at the center and root Of my heart of fire of hatred.

I worry that darkness is taken over. I still fight. I am filled with desire of darkness. So, I write these things So others can understand, Accept and Learn A different Perspective.

My goals in life are To go to all the holy places In the world to heal myself And Give new strength to my fight.

By Ally Brody

Forgotten Words

Find the thing which you have lost. Which is the same thing I have now. Remember, Acceptance is the key

To Knowledge and understanding. I have accepted what and Who I am though I don't know what I am but I do know who I am.

So, I have the key And want to entrust it to you. So, remember what I've said And the key will be yours.

Your wolf.

By Ally Brody

Forgotten Vision

Time is short. But I must know. Show me Visions of future.
One stands out from the rest. I will not tell them to anyone.
This vision I just hope won't come true. Maybe vision won't
come true But something tells me it will.

By Ally Brody

Forgotten Changes

My body knows the changes That are coming unto my
heart. The color of my eyes is a pale blue. They use to be a
darker, very deep blue. Changes come more rapidly now.
But, only I know what those changes are.

By Ally Brody

Forgotten Thoughts

This is not journal. This is not diary. Letters to mom To help her understand. To help her find Her own key that she lost.

These things, These dreams that are real. The Visions that I see. The wind tells me. I hear the wind. Comfort me wolves. Scary evil hunts me. Tempts me, my vampire love.

By Ally Brody

Forgotten Paths

The paths we take are our own. Everybody takes different paths. So, let me take my own path now.

By Ally Brody

Forgotten Plea

Please help me, Keep my wild instinct. Please help me look for it. Please help me go to the path That will help me find it again. I am losing my wild instinct, Please help me.

By Ally Brody

Forgotten Message

Split between two ways. One dark, one light. Darkness has wolves, Full moons, Love eternal, Eternal love, My love, And vampires. Light has fire spirits–Holy Spirit, God, My brother–Jesus, And radiant love.

By Ally Brody

Forgotten Summons

Come to me Ancient Darkness, Come to me Ancient Light For I am split between you two! Ancient Darkness cover the sky! Ancient Light come from the sky In a lightning flash!

My love awake from your slumber. My love open your eyes. My love come to me. Find me, my love. Look for me, my love.

I will never stop loving you. My love. My only. My one. I am yours. You are mine. We are one. My love make my eyes As sharp in the darkness As yours.

Come, brother thunder. Come to me. Come tell me, Is my love coming to me? Come, sister lightning. Come to me. Come tell me, Is my love coming to me?

Mother Make me damned. Brother Make me blessed.

By Ally Brody

Forgotten Decision

My love calls to me, But I need my brother And God to bless My decision. Forgive me, lord For what I must do.

By Ally Brody

Forgotten Oath

Blood of my blood, I will not harm. Flesh of my flesh, I will protect. Friendships that will last, I will not harm. Friends that will last, I will protect.

By Ally Brody

Forgotten Looking

To find my spirit which is lost. To find my soul which is lost. To find my heart which is lost. I know where to look. I need someone I trust to go with me.

Tired I am during the day. Awake I am in the night. I go to look in each castle For the scent of my love.

With the one I trust The ancient knowledge to. For when I am lost To the knowledge. I can go to the one And ask to teach me Back the knowledge I lost.

By Ally Brody

Forgotten Spell

Holy blood is holy wine. Holy flesh is holy bread. Holy wine is holy water.

By Ally Brody

Forgotten Keeping

To find where my love sleeps And awaken him. To keep a promise to my mother. To keep praising God and his son. To keep my connection with nature.

By Ally Brody

Forgotten Incantation

Noscia, contina Moniata Jesu Contaja Hitaja Monaja hisa. Sacre Espiritu *Hekiye monita hesa.*

Translation:

Hail, Holy Sister of Lord Jesus Who continues to protect us. Holy, Sacred Spirit Watch over us.

41

By Ally Brody

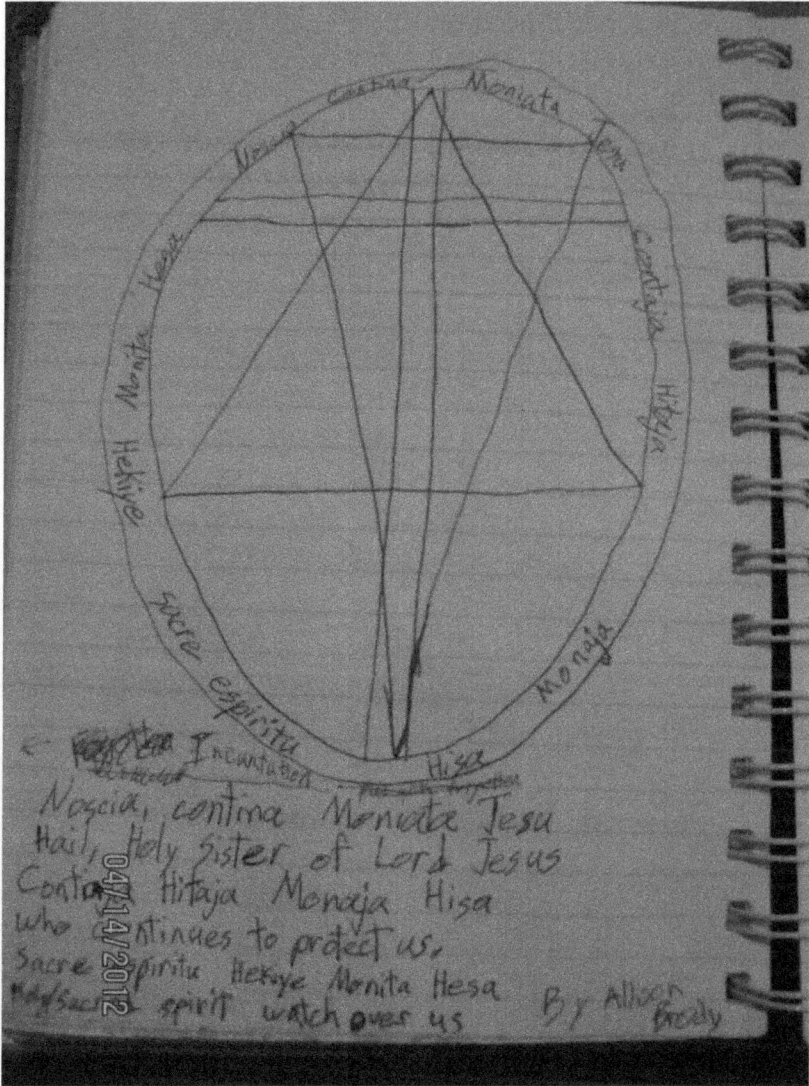

Seal of Protection By Allison E. Brody aka A.E.B.

College COP 2006 Series

Truly Christian

To be truly Christian, It means to be kind and caring To be completely spiritual.

By Ally Brody

Storm

To see it, To feel it. To know trouble is coming. It is coming for me because I have Dangerous knowledge. Where is the sun with its warmth as A symbol of God's love?

The clouds are blocking it, Making it cold and hopeless.

Where are the stars and The moon with their light As symbols of God's love Shining in the darkness?

The clouds cover them making It dark and despairing.

By Ally Brody

Looking

Looking for a mate, Looking for freedom, Looking to be complete, Looking for rest

By Ally Brody

Found

Have found God in nature Found spirits everywhere Listen to the wind and it will tell you things

By Ally Brody

Morning

Rays of light rise up from the darkness To shine in the sky and show no clouds that are near To block out the warmth of God's love

By Ally Brody

Sunset

Light and shadows mixing Clouds blocking the sun but light shines through. Oh! What a wondrous sight a sunset is As a creation of God.

By Ally Brody

Hope

Morning Cloudy, despairing, rainy. Afternoon, Shadows and light mix, Clouds breaking, Sky and sun coming through. Sunset, Sun shining, Light and shadows mixing Colors playing off the snow

By Ally Brody

Personal Belief and Morality

Personal belief Values Of living and of religion.

Spiritually, physically and much more Morality Values Of personal belief.

By Ally Brody

Christ's Love and Presence

Christ's love and presence Is everywhere In the trees, In the wind, In nature, In the elements, In the animals, And in the way people show that They love and care for each other.

By Ally Brody

Song Messages

Destiny

Things aren't always as they seem. The time comes when secrets are revealed. Listen to the wind and it will tell you that:

My death is coming and with it any protection in the world ends. The great storm is near. Armageddon is near.

The sun's warmth is the warmth of God's love To all his children that Are in the light. The star's light and the moon's light Are the light of God's love shining and waiting To lead the Rest of God's children that are In the darkness back to him.

I Walk a Path of light Deeper into the darkness And No one can change my destiny. My destiny Is Death. My fate is Greater than Anyone Knows.

By Ally Brody

Heart Messages

Alone

To find you there in my heart. When I sing it is as you're right beside me, But when I look around it saddens me, To find that you are not there.

Come to me wherever you are. Find me waiting for you. Crying silent tears, alone. When I am in bed going to sleep. They are only for you.

Let us see and comfort each other, In the darkness that Is gentle and calm filled with Pain, sadness and sorrow.

This darkness comforts me, When I am alone it reminds me of your presence. Will you Come and find me wherever I am and go?

If you will, please take me with you, And never leave me alone again. I am so Alone.

Come break this shell Around my heart that I made when I became indifferent To Most things to protect myself.

I'm dying inside. I'm half-alive, Half-dead Since I became indifferent. My heart is suffocating in loneliness. Will you come and free me?

No one is lonelier than me, Those who say that nobody cares for them, Don't see the people who care. But for me I know people care.

But they can't break this shell. Only you can. My love. My mate. My hell hound. Only you can destroy it completely, And know the secrets that I hide while Believing and understanding me.

Please help me live again. Be the bringer of my death. Be the bringer of my rebirth. Complete me. I feel so numb. Please let me feel again. Once you have me, Don't leave me. I don't want to be alone anymore.

Be the bringer of my death, I can't commit suicide. *I have to die protecting the people I love.* Be the bringer of my rebirth,I have a deal to fulfill with *Mind and body as His payment.*

My mother damns me. *Mother forgive me.* My brother blesses me. I walk a path of Light *Deeper into The darkness.* With only Nature, music, and animals To Comfort me. For I am the Holy sister of Nature, And I am a Wolf.

Two souls. Many spirits. I follow my heart. A human soul, *A demonic soul.* Human soul is dominate. Demonic soul is waiting to be awakened.

I listen to nature. I listen from The trees, waters, Earth, air, and animals. I listen to nature. Listen to what the wind has to say. Can you hear it? It says:

The great storm is coming. The apocalypse is near. My death is near. For when I die, There will be no protection. It will begin.

My family is worthy of me. My friends are worthy of me. Everyone that cares for and loves me is worthy of me. And yet I am not worthy of them.

As great as I am spiritually, I am nothing physically. I want to die. But I want to live to protect my pack. Into depression for my family and pack's sake. For depression is just anger turned inward, And I would never intentionally hurt The ones I care about and love.

If I said that No one loves or cares for me, Then I would be lying because I see. Yet I tell the truth when I say that No one is Alone wolf like me except one person. I tell the truth and yet sometimes I don't. But always when Spirituality is the subject, I tell the truth always.

So alone, Don't want to be Alone anymore. I am dying, Make me live. Want to die, Want to live. Walk a path of light Deeper into the darkness.

Mother damns me. Mother loves me. Mother curses me. Brother forgives me. When I die it will be protecting my pack. If mother dies before me then I'll kill myself to save her soul. If I die before mother then She will understand.

I bring life. I bring death. I bring happiness. I bring sorrow. I am alone, unique, and burden. No one should bare what I have to burden.

I am alone envying others on Having a person to love That Is not family or friends. I am tired Please let me sleep. I don't want to be alone anymore.

By Ally Brody

Alone II

To find you there in my heart. When I sing, it is as you're right beside me. But when I look around it saddens me To find that you are not there.

Come to me wherever you are. Find me waiting for you. Crying silent tears, alone. When I am in bed going to sleep. They are only for you.

Let us see and comfort each other, In the darkness that is gentle and calm, Filled with pain, sadness and sorrow. This darkness comforts me, When I am alone it reminds me of your presence.

Will you Come and find me wherever I am and go? If you will, please take me with you, And never leave me alone again.

By Ally Brody

Lonely Heart

I am so alone. Come and break this shell around

my heart that I made When I became indifferent to most things to protect myself.

I am dying inside. I am Half-alive, Half-dead. Since I became indifferent. My heart is suffocating in loneliness. Will you come and free me?

No one is lonelier than me. Those who say that nobody cares, Don't see the people that do.

I know people care but they can't break this shell. Only you can destroy it completely, And know the secrets that I hide While Believing and understanding me.

Please help me live again. Be the bringer of my death, The bringer of my rebirth. Complete me. I feel so numb. Please let me feel again. I don't want to be alone anymore.

By Ally Brody

Split Heart

Two souls Combined within one. I follow my heart. An angelic soul, A demonic soul. A human soul. Angelic and human Souls are dominant. Demonic soul is waiting to be awakened.

I listen to nature. I listen from the trees, waters, earth, air, and animals. Listen to what the wind has to say.

Can you hear it? It says, *The great storm is coming. The apocalypse is near. My death is near.* For when I die, There will be no protection. When that happens it will begin.

By Ally Brody

Protection Oath

When I die it will be protecting my family. If mother dies I'll kill myself to save her soul. If I die before her then she will understand.

By Ally Brody

What I bring

I bring life. I bring death. I bring happiness. I bring sorrow. I am alone, unique and burdened. No one should bear what I have to burden.

I am alone envying others on having Someone to love that is not family or friends. I am tired. Please I need sleep. I don't want to be alone anymore.

By Ally Brody

Being Worthy

My family is worthy of me. My friends are worthy of me. Everyone that cares and loves me is worthy of me,

And yet I am not worthy of them. As great as I am spiritually, I am nothing physically.

I'm so alone. I want to die. But I need to live to protect my family. Into depression for my family and pack's sake. For depression is just anger turned inward,

And I would never intentionally hurt the ones I care about and love.

If I said that no one loves or cares for or about me. Then I would be lying because I see. Yet I tell the truth when I say, No one is a lone wolf like me except one.

I tell the truth and yet sometimes I don't. But always when Spirituality is the subject, I tell the truth always.

By Ally Brody

Split Soul

I don't want to be alone anymore. I'm dying inside, Make me live. I want to die, Want to live. I walk a path of light, Deeper into the darkness.

Mother damns me, Brother blesses me. Mother is afraid of me, Mother loves me. Mother curses me, Brother blesses me. Mother damns me, Brother forgives me. Mother please forgive me.

By Ally Brody

Horses

Loving, Bratty, Strength, Guardians of Earth

By Ally Brody

Cats

Mysterious, Curious, Unpredictable, Lovable, Guardians of the sun

By Ally Brody

Wolves

Calm, Protective, Family oriented, Guardians of the forest and the moon

By Ally Brody

Ravens

Mystery, Death, New life, Knowledge, Carriers of spirits, Guardians of the sky and moon

By Ally Brody

Squirrel

East, Gathering, Preparation, Greatest spiritual challenge

By Ally Brody

Dog

South, Loyal, Noble, Teaching Of true and loyal friends, Protects the child within

By Ally Brody

Swan

West, Grace, Peace, Elegance, Purity, Innocence, Leads to Personal truth, Inner answers, Show path to goals

By Ally Brody

Opossum

North, Strategy, Grasping, Agility, Marital instinct, Stability, Diversion, Wise counsel

By Ally Brody

Moose

Above, Self-esteem, Authority, Warrior, Balance, Fearlessness

By Ally Brody

Turtle

Below, Mother Earth, Retreat, Toughness, Inner earth, Grounded

By Ally Brody

Coyote

Within, Trickster, Wise fool, Wisdom-keeper, Find heart's joy, Faithful to personal truth

By Ally Brody

Wolf

Right side, Teacher, Guardian, Courage, Warrior spirit, Family

By Ally Brody

Snake

Left side, Transmutation, Healing, Power of creation

By Ally Brody

Eagle

Spirit, Vision, Messenger Of The Great Spirit God

By Ally Brody

Mountain Lion

Leadership, Courage, Foresight, Strength

By Ally Brody

Armadillo

Boundaries, Teach me my shield, To reflect hurt, So I will not yield

By Ally Brody

Whale

Record keeper, Soul's path, Secrets of ages, Within your call, Roots of history

By Ally Brody

Dolphin

Manna, Breath of the Divine, Oneness, Playfulness, Communication, Community, Guidance

By Ally Brody

Raccoon

Generous protector, Resourcefulness, Protector

By Ally Brody

Frog

Cleaning, Purification, Singing, Rainmaker

By Ally Brody

Antelope

Action, Decisiveness, Speed, Sacrifice

By Ally Brody

Lizard

Dreaming, Dreamtime, Visions, Ancient

By Ally Brody

Blue Heron

Self-reflection, Sacred water bird, Power of knowing, Reflecting spirits, Eternal goal

By Ally Brody

Spider

Weaving, Creation

By Ally Brody

Grouse

Sacred spiral, Personal power

By Ally Brody

Jaguar

Integrity, Impeccability, Compassion

By Ally Brody

Hawk

Messenger, Focus, Perspective, Detachment, Swiftness

By Ally Brody

Fox

Camouflage, Adaptability, Shape-shifting, Cunning,
Protector of the family unit

By Ally Brody

Horse

Power, Freedom, Compromise

By Ally Brody

Owl

Deception, Omens, Wisdom, Shadows, Magic, Sacred medicine bird

By Ally Brody

Weasel

Stealth, Loner, Powerful ally

By Ally Brody

Prairie Dog

Retreat, Rest, Replenish

By Ally Brody

Bat

Rebirth, Birth, Death, Journey of the soul

By Ally Brody

Mouse

Scrutiny, Sort, Detailed

By Ally Brody

Ant

Patience, Community, Planner

By Ally Brody

Crow

Law, Secret of balance, Left-handed guardian, Keeper of the sacred law, Master of illusion, Shape shifter

By Ally Brody

Deer

Gentleness, Pathfinder, Kindness, Purity

By Ally Brody

Giraffe

Foresight, Prophesy, Divination, Risk–taking

By Ally Brody

Kangaroo

Gratitude, Color, Vibration

By Ally Brody

Koala

Empathy, Safety, Sensitivity

By Ally Brody

Lion

Courage, Nobility, Dignity

By Ally Brody

Lynx

Secrets, Discernment, Inner vision

By Ally Brody

Porcupine

Innocence, Humility, Trust

By Ally Brody

Otter

Women medicine, Surrender, Family, Merging

By Ally Brody

Rabbit

Fear, Fertility, Sacrifice

By Ally Brody

Seal

Imagination, Creativity, Adaptation

By Ally Brody

Butterfly

Transformation, Vibrancy, Colorfulness, Reincarnation

By Ally Brody

Cougar

Confidence, Leadership, Conviction

By Ally Brody

Raven

Magic, Shadow, Insight, Prophecy, Shape-shifting

By Ally Brody

I am

I am like the squirrel For I am preparing for
Something that Has not happened yet. I am like the
dog For I am loyal To those I choose To be Loyal to. I
am like the swan For I am peaceful.

I am like the opossum For I create strategy For a few
situations. I am like the moose For I have and need
Self-esteem. I am like the turtle For sometimes I need
to retreat to Keep my strength.

I am like the coyote For some people Call me a fool In believing in Things they may not But I am a wise Fool. I am like the wolf Because I am a guardian To everyone I know And don't know. I am like the snake For I can heal and change.

I am like the eagle For I am a spirit And a messenger And I see Visions Which tell of Pasts that could have been And futures that could be. I am like the mountain lion For I have Courage to follow My heart and instincts.

I am like the armadillo For I have Placed boundaries Around my heart To block out Pain, anger, and sadness.

I am like the whale For I am a Record keeper In my own way, I take the soul's path, And I have Secrets of ages Hidden in my heart Where my soul lies. I am like the dolphin For I am playful.

I am like the raccoon For I am A generous protector
And Resourceful. I am like the frog For I like to sing
And I am a rainmaker. I am like the antelope For I like
to be decisive And I also sacrifice.

I am like the lizard For I Dream And Have visions And I
am ancient. I am like the blue heron For I Self-reflect
And I have The power of knowing In my heart.

I am like the spider For what I create In action, word,
or penmanship Is beautiful but also dangerous. I am
like the grouse For I have Great personal power. I am
like the jaguar For I have Compassion.

I am like the hawk For I am a messenger. I am like the
fox For I can adapt And I am The protector of my
family unit. I am like the horse For I have Power and
freedom Yet I can compromise.

I am like the owl For I have Wisdom and omens, And I can deceive. I am like the weasel For I have Stealth, I am a loner, And a powerful ally.

I am like the prairie dog For I retreat to prepare for The Journey ahead. I am like the bat For I am on A blind journey of the soul. I am like the mouse For I am very detailed.

I am like the ant For I have Patience. I am like the crow For I am Keeper of the sacred law And a master of illusion And I have The secrets of balance In my heart.

I am like the deer For I have Gentleness and kindness And I am a pathfinder. I am like the giraffe For I take Risks with The simplest things. I am like the kangaroo For I have Gratitude For the simplest things.

I am like the koala For I have Empathy for everything. I
am like the lion For I have Courage, nobility, and
dignity In everything I do Even if it does not show.

I am like the lynx For I have Secrets I Tell only to
Those Who cannot tell Without my Permission.

I am like the porcupine For I can have Humility, And
an innocent-like trust. I am like the otter For I can
Surrender or merge myself. I am like the rabbit For I
have fear And I can sacrifice.

I am like the seal For I have Imagination and creativity
And I can adapt. I am like the butterfly For I am the
last reincarnation. I am like the cougar For I have
Confidence.

I am like the raven For I have Insight, And prophecies
yet revealed; And we are both of Magic and shadow

By Ally Brody

Protection Messages- Three Times- July 2007

Three times three, A part of me. Three times three,
My heart will lead. Three times three, My heart will be.

By Ally Brody

Dream Series

Nightmare

The first time She remembers dreaming, Was at the
age of four or five. This is the nightmare that she
dreamed:

**She was in her bedroom at night, But she saw herself
in bed Sleeping on the right side. A demon's hand
comes up From under the bed Grabbing her left leg.**

When the demon touched her leg, She was back in her body. It swung her around in a circle for What seemed like five minutes.

She woke up screaming, Then running to her parents for safety. A boogeyman dream That came true as Physical pain in real life.

By Ally Brody

Soul Mate

The second time She dreamed was at the age of Eleven, twelve, or thirteen. She dreamed that:

She was in a bed in a house In a valley surrounded by mountains. She gets out of bed. Suddenly, she is outside in the village.

It is night. The moon is full. There is a mountain with a Castle on top of it. She feels drawn to it. She runs up the mountain towards the castle.

Suddenly, she is in the castle. She walks to where she feels pulled to. She meets a vampire. Suddenly, he is right in front of her. He takes her right hand. He bites her thumb as she wakes up.

One word that she remembers The vampire saying is "Changeling". When she writes down her dream saying:

Black is the clothes he wears. Red is the color of his eyes. Love, need, desire, and freedom is What his presence makes me feel. Nadayah is my nickname for the vampire.

By Ally Brody

Soul Mate by Allison E. Brody aka A.E.B.

Eternal Forgiveness

Her third dream, at age fifteen. While sleeping face down she dreamed that:

She was laying on her back On the ground in a clearing in a forest. It is nighttime with a full moon.

Her brother, Jesus Christ, is in the clearing with a wolf. They are talking about her. She looked directly at them, And the wolf disappears into the forest.

She heard the wind howling then she realized she couldn't feel the wind, and that it was wolves that were howling for her.

No, they were calling her. Her brother speaks and says;

You have our forgiveness and always will. Go to them. They are calling for you. Go, you have been away for far to long.

Then she wakes up. Her brother's presence makes her feel peaceful.

By Ally Brody

Vision of the End

The forth time She dreamed was at the age of 16. She dreamed a vision this time. This is what she envisioned:

She dreamed that **She was surrounded by darkness,**

And in her hands was a flame, Just a flame; no candle.

It consumed other flames of people, Who looked for her in the darkness, Until it consumed the brightest flame of all That the father, Her Brother, and her belonged to.

So, everyone was blinded when the light (Heaven) and the darkness (Hell) Emerged into one and the darkness was gone and there was just bright light And nothing else.

All throughout this vision dream, She felt just calm and indifference.

By Ally Brody

Snake Dream

When she had her fifth Dream, She was 20 years old. This is what she dreamed:

She was in a desert during the day. She saw a snake. She got closer. She saw it was a cobra. She felt the need to help it.

She picked it up three times. Each time she picked it up,The cobra bit her on her right arm. Each time she drops it.

On the third time, She falls to the ground lying face up. She knows that the venom is working, that she is dying.

She wakes up still feeling the venom working in her arm. She lays there waiting for what ever may happen. The feeling goes up her arm to a point, Then it slowly recedes and dissipates.

All through this dream she feels the need to help.

By Ally Brody

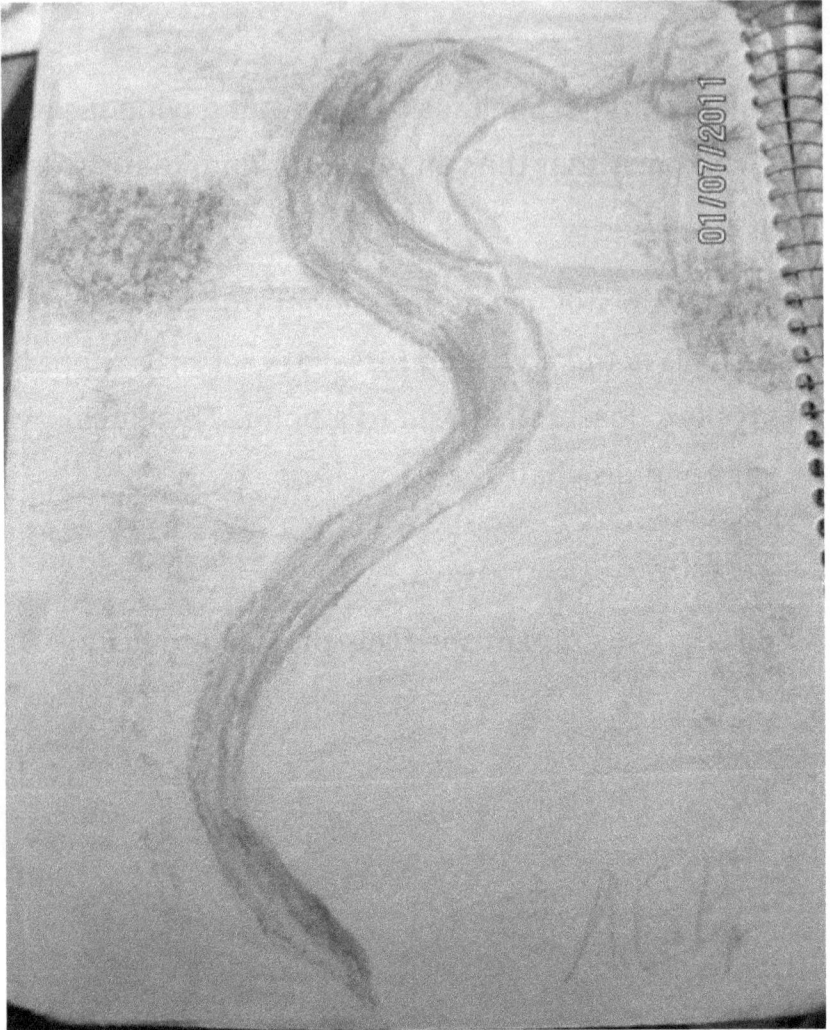

Snake Rose by Allison E Brody aka A.E.B.

Island Dream

She had her fifth dream at the age of 23. And this is what she dreamt:

She is on an island by the ocean. She is with people (she doesn't recognize any).

They start to play a game with a ball then it turns into a race across islands and ocean, Through caves with rocks to climb, and over waterfalls without stopping.

Some of the people are swimming, and others have motorboats. She is swimming fast and gets ahead. Through obstacles she goes without getting stopped or taking a breath. Someone says to her something like, *You're doing great, Keep going.*

Somehow she starts to imagine herself, in the dream, a shark. At the final obstacle, she gets caught and scratched, and she tries to get out, then she wakes up.

All throughout the dream she felt free then at the end she felt caught.

By Ally Brody

Doubts of the Heart (written in 2004)

As time goes on and darkness grows, Will I ever see the three loves that have three pieces of my heart?

I, of whom I cannot live without all three loves. As my mind and heart wander, I have begun to doubt my heart. But do I doubt that which I follow?

I will never know the truth until I am hypnotized. But what do I say at night in mumbles?

I know I have to find out. I have a plan. But this is only the second thing I am sure of in my life.

By Ally Brody

If You have any

Comments or Questions,

Please Contact Me

on my website:

www.cernuwolfraven.com

or

at brodyae@gmail.com